Newcastle: Past and Pres

Geoff Phillips

Special Edition

Published by G P Electronic Services
87 Willowtree Avenue
Durham
DH1 1DZ
Tel: 091 384 9707

First published 1990
Revised and re-printed 1994

ISBN 0 9522480 1 8

Front cover design, interior design and graphics by Geoff Phillips.

Present day photographs by Craig Oliphant.

Printed by:
Smith Print Group Limited, Sutherland House, South Shore Road, Gateshead. Tel: 091 490 1001

The Jack Phillips Photograph Collection

This book features photographs from my late father's collection of photographs of Newcastle upon Tyne as it was in days gone by. Some of the photographs date back to the 1840's which is when photography was in its infancy.

Jack Phillips was born in Bishop Auckland, Co Durham in 1910 and was one of a family of five brothers and sisters. His father was a postman with Bishop Auckland GPO and Jack followed in his father's footsteps by joining the Post Office as a telegraph boy in 1924. In six years he graduated to postman and worked at post offices in Stockton, Thornaby, and Whitley Bay for fourteen years until he was retired from the GPO due to a duodenal ulcer. He always regarded his imposed retirement as most unfair as his complaint did not affect his work to any significant degree. After working for the Home & Counties Tea Company for a while, in 1939 he was called up to join the Territorial Army at Gosforth Park as a motorbike despatch rider.

When the war was over, Jack took up a post as costing clerk with C A Parsons, the steam turbine manufacturer of Byker, a suburb of Newcastle upon Tyne. A few years later he married and lived in a flat on Shields Road in Byker. He took a great interest in the history of Newcastle and started collecting old photographs, sketches and historical notes on the City. His collection was greatly augmented when he was given a collection of rare prints of views of Newcastle by a retired doctor from Jesmond. The doctor had been a collector himself for many years and wanted his collection to be adopted by a serious enthusiast. Many of the prints were in poor condition and Jack arranged for them to be copied so that negatives were produced for further printing of the photographs.

In the 1950's and 1960's Jack spent many Sunday mornings walking around the streets of Newcastle, trying to discover the locations of the old photographs and, with the help of a photographer friend, he set about taking new photographs of the old views so as to produce a "then and now" pair of pictures. His old Newcastle photographs appeared regularly in the Newcastle Evening Chronicle newspaper and Northern Life magazine and he gave exhibitions of his collection at Harkers of Grainger Street and Lockhart's Neville Street restaurant for their diamond jubilee celebration in 1951. Displays of his photographs were often seen in the canteen of C A Parsons and he Liaised closely with the staff of the local studies department of Newcastle upon Tyne's Central Library. He was often called upon to show parties of visitors around the historical parts of the city.

Jack Phillips died of cancer in February 1986 at the age of 75, leaving a unique pictorial record of the streets and buildings of Newcastle upon Tyne and its suburbs. I have prepared this book in memory of my father and so that many more people can view and enjoy some of the photographs from his collection.

Past and Present

One of the most fascinating aspects of Jack's collection was the Past and Present pairs of photographs where he attempted to replicate the same camera angles as the early shots, and wherever possible include a point of reference which could be used as a link between the old and new photographs. When my father died, I took an interest in his collection and realised that many of his "Present" views which had been taken in the 1950's and 1960's had changed again and were now "Old Newcastle". I decided to embark on phase three of the project and arranged to take the views again in the 1990's. In some cases all three photographs have been included in this presentation where the changes are pronounced. In two instances it has been possible to show four photographs of the same scene. In most cases there is an obvious link between the old and new photographs of the same view but sometimes the links are hard to find and searching for them adds to the reader's enjoyment of the book.

Replicating the same camera angles as the early photographs was not an easy task. The angle of the original camera lens was sometimes difficult to duplicate and in some cases a building occupied the spot where the original cameraman stood. In 1860 it was probably quite safe for the photographer to set up his tripod in the middle of the street but not in the 1990's. In order to get the correct angle, the 1990's cameraman sometimes risked life and limb waiting for a gap in the traffic and then stood in the middle of the street while the author acted as look-out for approaching cars. Street signs, traffic lights and parked vehicles were also a problem which forced the modern cameraman to use a different vantage point. The early cameras were fitted with bellows which enabled the photographer to tilt the lens in such a way so as to correct the distortion which gave the effect that the buildings were leaning over. The early photographs, taken with a wide angle lens showed all the buildings perfectly vertical. In general, a modern camera fitted with a similar lens cannot compensate for this effect and consequently there is a strange list to the buildings in some of the modern photographs. Some correction was possible during the printing and enlarging process however.

The Jack Phillips Hawaiian Band at Gosforth Assembly Rooms in 1956

Jack Phillips - the Musician

Jack's other passion was music. He played the Hawaiian guitar in his own band and supplied music for dancing at venues thoughout the North-East. Jack is seen in the centre of the photograph above at the Gosforth Assembly Rooms supplying the music at a dinner dance for C A Parsons' transformer drawing office staff. Joe Hanley is playing the drums and Horsley Hall is on piano. Horsley is also a keen historian specialising in Tyneside's past.

1.(a) Quayside c.1928

This fascinating photograph shows the Quayside of Newcastle upon Tyne in about 1928 and shows that in those days it was a busy port. The man on the right is having engine trouble and probably wishes he had stuck with a horse and cart.

(b) 1990's

Every Sunday the Quayside is the venue for a market where all sorts of merchandise is on sale and many a bargain may be had.

2.(a) Side 1880

The street called Side was probably so-named because it ran up the side of the castle. For centuries traffic crossing the old Tyne Bridge would have to negotiate this steep and narrow street to reach the centre of the city. In 1787 a new route was built called Dean Street which followed the course of the Lort Burn; a stream which ran into the River Tyne.

(b) 1952

Milburn House replaces the old buildings on the right of the 1880 photograph. The buildings on the left are shored up and seem ready for demolition. There is an interesting link between the 1880 and 1952 shots.

(c) 1990's

The only building to stand the test of time is St. Nicholas House in the centre of the photograph which has survived the 100 years since the first photograph.

3.(a) Black Gate and Keep   1895

The Black Gate was the main entrance to the castle of Newcastle upon Tyne. The Black Gate was built by King Henry III in 1248, about 70 years after the completion of the Keep and other parts of the fortress. The upper section of the Black Gate was added in the early part of the 17th century when it was converted into a dwelling. The Keep is on the right of the photograph and it is the structure which gave Newcastle its name. The first Norman castle was built by Robert Curthose the eldest son of William the Conqueror and was probably a wooden fort. The new castle which gave the town its name was built from stone by Henry II from about 1168 onwards; it cost £892 18s 9d, and it is this structure which stands today.

(b) 1990's

Little has changed since the 1895 view. The Black Gate has been kept in good condition by the Society of Antiquaries who undertook major restoration work in the late nineteenth century. The Society now uses the building as a museum. The Keep is maintained by the City and is open to visitors. There are excellent views of Newcastle and Gateshead from its towers.

4.(a) High Level Bridge   1885

The High Level Bridge was built by Robert Stephenson between 1846 and 1849, and constructed from cast iron and stone. The engine perched on the top is Stephenson's "Billy" which was used at Killingworth Colliery but is now in the Stephenson's Railway Museum at Middle Engine Lane in the north-east suburbs of Newcastle.

(b) 1950's

A new Bridge Hotel has been built having graduated from an inn to an hotel.

(c) 1990's

A weight limit has been placed on the roadway section of the bridge which is now showing signs of deterioration. The structure was so well designed however, that it is able to carry modern railway rolling stock on its upper level with ease.

5.(a) Westgate Road / Collingwood Street   1904

In 1904 it was possible to walk in the middle of the street without the fear of being knocked down by motor vehicles.   Barclays Bank is under construction on the left and W R Pape's premises are shown on the right. Mr Pape was the inventor and patentee of breech loading guns and rifles.

(b) 1990's

It still looks as though one could walk safely in the middle of the road today, but even though the photograph was taken on a Sunday morning, the cameraman had to wait several minutes for a gap in the traffic. The fine building constructed for Barclays Bank is now a night club.

6.(a) Clayton Street / Pink Lane   1890

This view shows John Knox Church, designed by John Dobson; the famous architect who designed many fine buildings and streets for the city. John Knox was a sixteenth century Scottish Protestant reformer who founded the Church of Scotland. The John Knox Church is now in Elswick Road. Pink Lane which leads to the Central Station is at the extreme left of the photograph.

(b) 1960

John Knox Church has been demolished and replaced by Clarendon House. The high class tobacconist H Sigar sells cigars on the corner.

(c) 1990's

The list of the buildings on the left is due to the camera lens and not the reason for the scaffolding.

7.(a) Clayton Street   1915

This view is looking north and is at the junction with Westgate Road. Even though the policeman is on point duty, he still has time to chat to a local workman. Cinemas were very popular in the early 1900's and the Picture House on the right was one of the first cinemas in Newcastle. The aerial objects are the interconnecting pieces of the tram wires.

(b) 1990's

The Picture House has been replaced by a bingo hall although this building used to be the Majestic dance hall a favourite haunt of 1950's and 60's youth. The remaining buildings were constructed by Grainger and remain largely unchanged. Sadly this part of the city is becoming run-down and some of the shops are boarded up. Many of the shops which are trading are "money-stretcher" bargain stores.

8.(a) Grainger Street   1890

This street was named after Richard Grainger who built many of Newcastle's finest streets and buildings. The medieval St. John's Church is on the right and the horse-drawn tram is heading towards the Central Station. The tram's hoarding is advertising the local pharmacist, Inman.

(b) 1990's

The horse-drawn trams have been replaced by a fleet of mini-buses. The City planners have retained the line of this fine street by fitting the street lighting to the stone buildings, thus avoiding intrusive lamp standards. St. John's Church has stood the test of time as it is said that parts of the church were built as early as 1130; the tower was added in 1230.

9.(a) Fenkle Street   1898

The large building on the left was Cross House which was the mansion of an important townsman of the eighteenth century. In the nineteenth century it was used as a vicarage to St. John's Church but was later turned into business premises.

(b) 1990's

The original Cross House was destroyed in 1919 by a terrible fire caused by the ignition of movie film which was stored in the basement. The new Cross House dominates the view of the 1990's shot.

10.(a) Westgate Road / Lockhart's Cocoa Rooms   1895

The policy of Mr Robert Lockhart when he first introduced his cocoa rooms to Liverpool in 1876, was to give the best possible value for money. His son-in-law, Mr H Crawford, opened these budget-priced restaurants in Newcastle, and they quickly gained popularity with the townspeople. The cocoa rooms were welcomed by many as a more desirable alternative to the drunken atmosphere of public houses, and Mr Lockhart himself was keenly interested in the temperance movement.

(b) 1990's

The cocoa rooms have long since disappeared but were the forerunners of the Carricks chain of food stores. One of the new shops is a dealer in t.v. items (although that doesn't stand for television and I don't think the patrons of the cocoa rooms would have approved)

11.(a) Blackfriars   1880

Originally a Dominican friary founded in the thirteenth century.   After the dissolution of the monasteries in 1539, the buildings passed to the town council who rented them to the trade guilds. During the nineteenth and twentieth centuries, Blackfriars fell into disrepair.

(b) 1990's

Fortunately the buildings were restored in the 1970's. A restaurant has been placed in the priory's refectory and several small craft workshops surround the cloisters.

12.(a) Newgate Street / White Cross   1960's

In the 1970's much of Newcastle's city centre was demolished to make way for the Eldon Square shopping complex. This shot shows some of the shops that were present before it was built. The cross in the middle of the road marks the spot where a market square with a spire called the White Cross once stood.

(b) 1990's

A multi-storey car park now dominates the view and the street has been widened to accommodate a bus station. We are now able to see into Percy Street from this angle. The position of the White Cross is now denoted by a cross of white stones in the traffic island in the foreground although this is difficult to see in the photograph.

13.(a) Bigg Market

Bigg is a type of coarse barley which farmers brought to this part of the town to sell. The tall building on the right was Newcastle's town hall until the 1960's when the council moved to the new Civic Centre at Barras Bridge. Notice another of Lockhart's cocoa rooms.

(b) 1990's

This area is still used as a market on certain days of the week but the produce on sale is more interesting than coarse barley. Many of the buildings in the early shot are still standing today. The Bigg Market is now a popular haunt of young people in the evening who are attracted by the many pubs and restaurants there.

14.(a) Newgate Street   1911

The building in the centre of the photograph is the Empire Palace theatre which played host to many famous entertainers and acts. The London Philharmonic Orchestra performed there in 1940, as did the Beatles in the early 1960's, supporting the Everly Brothers. The theatre was closed in 1963 and demolished two years later.

(b) 1990's

Although the Empire Palace has gone, the Rose and Crown next door continues to do business. The Swallow Hotel and the Newgate Shopping Precinct now dominate the view.

15.(a) Clayton Street East 1   1920

Clayton Street used to continue eastwards and join up with Blackett Street. At the end of Clayton Street was the fish market and the bird market and on the right of the picture is the Grainger Market.

(b) 1990's

Today, the buildings on the left form part of Eldon Square's Green Market. Clayton Street is now blocked off by more of the Square just beyond Nelson Street. Grainger Market is still in existence on the right.

16.(a) Clayton Street East 2   1915

This photograph was taken very near to the previous shot and shows the Cambridge public house in the centre. Further to the left, an employee of Mr Lockhart has stopped work for a while to observe the photographer, and the lady upstairs is also curious to know what is going on.

(b) 1990's

The main structure of the buildings is unchanged but none of the original traders remains.

17.(a) Corner Newgate Street / Low Friar Street   1879

A bright sunny day and the Three Tuns Inn is not yet open for business. There were many public houses in Newcastle upon Tyne and some brewed their own beer on the premises.

(b) 1990's

It is hard to believe that the two pictures were taken from the same spot but if you look very carefully you will find a link between the old and new photographs.

18.(a) Darn Crook 1890

Meaning obscure or crooked street, Darn Crook's name was changed by the time of the second shot to St. Andrews Street, after the church on the right. It seems as though advertising agents could place their posters anywhere they wished without any regard to the aesthetics of the city's buildings. The poster in the foreground is appropriate as Andrews' Liver Salts were actually invented in Newcastle upon Tyne.

(b) 1990's

The tall building in the distance with a star is part of the Newcastle Breweries where the world famous Brown Ale is brewed and exported to over forty different countries. The Newcastle Co-operative Stores are on the left.

19.(a) Top of Darn Crook   1890's

This picture was taken at the top of Darn Crook looking south towards Newgate Street. Darn Crook only ran as far as the town wall until 1810 when it was extended to meet up with Gallowgate. The windmill was damaged by fire early in the nineteenth century and was demolished in 1896.

(b) 1950's
This photograph shows part of the town wall on the left.

(c) 1990's
Little has changed since the 1950's although the cars just don't seem to be as stylish as in the previous picture.

20.(a) Green Market   c.1900

The Green Market was where traders who were not fortunate enough to own their own premises, could market their fruit and vegetables. St. Andrews' churchyard may be seen at the right of the picture

(b) 1990's

Fruit and vegetable merchants would find it rather hazardous using this site today. Cameras certainly created more interest at the turn of the century than now. There is a link between the two photographs.

21. Corner Percy Street / Gallowgate 1

(a) 1895

The shops on the right hand side of the picture were built in 1706. The building in the centre housed the premises of Mr. T Howe, funeral director.

(b) 1960

In 1960 the old shops are still there as is Mr Howe's, although the hoarding has gone and the establishment now furnishes "brighter homes". Notice the wires overhead which carried the electric power for Newcastle's trolley buses.

(c) 1966

The shops have gone despite efforts to save them; they were finally demolished to make way for the IBM building and Barclay's Bank. It is a pity that John Dobson was not around to design a better building than this.

(d) 1990's

Little has changed between the last two shots but the absence of the trolley bus wires gives a much cleaner view. Traffic lights have been replaced by a mini-round-about.

22.(a) Corner Percy Street / Blackett Street   1920

The King's Head pub remained until the 1970's when it was pulled down to build the Eldon Square shopping complex. Notice the toddler on the right; it is doubtful whether a mother would allow a small child to play without supervision on Blackett Street today.

(b) 1990's

The new Lloyds Bank on the left forms part of the Eldon Square complex and is quite an impressive building having much more character than Barclay's premises across the street. Despite increased awareness of architecture, the best the city can come up with to straddle Blackett Street is the child's building block structure seen on the right.

23.(a) Corner Percy Street / Gallowgate 2   1895

This is the same corner as view No 21 but taken from a different angle. It gives a clearer view of the eighteenth century shops which were nearly two hundred years old when the photograph was taken.

(b) 1990's

There is no link between the two photographs but views 21 (a) to (d) confirm that they are the same view.

24.(a) Percy Street   c.1880

The building at the top left was the Jewish synagogue on Leazes Park Road and was built in 1880. A local resident lets her dog out for a few minutes at the end of the day.

(b) 1987

The building on the right was part of Handyside Arcade which was nick-named Arcadia during the swinging 60's. The building housed the legendary Club-a-Go Go where the famous Newcastle band "The Animals" played.

(c) 1990's

This photograph was taken soon before the Leazes Arcade was burned down. The new buildings in the centre are part of Eldon Gardens, an extension to the Eldon Square shopping complex.

25.(a) Farmer's Rest, Haymarket   1890

This remarkable photograph shows the well know Newcastle pub in 1890. It was an apt name for a pub in the Haymarket as it was where many farmers came to sell their produce.

(b) 1920

By 1920 a smart new building had been erected which housed the Newcastle Breweries as well as the Farmer's Rest Hotel. The building is typical of the type of public house built in the early part of the twentieth century.

(c) 1990's

The pub now seems choked by the bus station, its traffic and the general chaos of the 1990's lifestyle.

26.(a) Haymarket   1904

In 1824 this area was established as a market for hay and straw, but was later used as a stand for horse cabs. St. Thomas's Church on the right, designed by John Dobson, was built in 1830 as a replacement for St. Thomas's Chapel which was demolished in 1828. It was built on the site of the Mary Magdalene Leper Hospital. On the extreme left of the picture is the Grand Hotel built in 1890 by James Deuchar.

(b) 1975

The most prominent feature in the Haymarket in 1975 was the South African War Memorial, built in memory of the soldiers who died in the Boer War. The tower of Newcastle's Civic Centre completed in 1967 is seen just to the right of the lamp standard.

(c) 1990's

In the final photograph the Haymarket Metro station almost obscures the original view. The angel on the top of the memorial was temporarily removed in case of damage while drilling operations for the Metro took place.

27.(a) Haymarket Public House

PERCY ST. NEWCASTLE.

The pub is shown on the right of the picture and it is believed that it was the eighteenth century home of a policeman called Nixon. The house was converted into a pub in 1833.

(b) 1990's

A group of Newcastle students and locals tried in vain to prevent its demolition but 1987 saw its demise for the sake of extra car parking spaces for the University. The Newcastle Breweries building to the left of the site of the pub has managed to escape the bulldozer.

28.(a) Barras Bridge   1906

This photograph shows Mr Phillips' (no relation) food store on Barras Bridge on July 11 1906, the date of the visit to Newcastle by King Edward VII. It is thought that the name Barras Bridge may be a corruption of Barriers Bridge, a bridge at the barriers of the town.

(b) 1950's

The author is seen (a little younger than he is today) posing reluctantly for the photographer who is taking the same view nearly 50 years later.
Mr Phillips seems to have moved to the shop on the right.

(c) 1990's

All the buildings have been demolished for extra car parking spaces for the University of Newcastle upon Tyne. The Newcastle Playhouse theatre may now be seen from Barras Bridge.

29.(a) Northumberland Road   1910

The White City building was originally opened as a skating rink. It then became the home of Ginnet's Circus and later the Hippodrome cinema. The original Olympia was built in 1893 but was destroyed by fire in 1907. The Olympia cinema shown here was built in 1909; the first "talkie" to be shown there was "Broadway Melody".

(b) 1966

The Olympia was still standing in 1966 and to the left are the distinctive premises of Rossleigh's garage. The new building in the centre is part of Newcastle Polytechnic (now the University of Northumbria).

(c) 1990's

A new street called John Dobson Street now cuts across Northumberland Road where Rossleigh's garage once stood. An NCP car park has replaced the Olympia.

30.(a) Fenwick's Store, Northumberland Street   1920

Mr J J Fenwick opened his first Newcastle store in 1882 and soon established a reputation for retailing high quality clothes. Northumberland Street was and still is the most popular shopping street in Newcastle and Mr Fenwick's business went from strength to strength.

(b) 1990's

The store was rebuilt in 1923. In the 1950's Fenwick employed musicians to play in the restaurant at lunchtime and it was considered the place to be "seen in". The author can particularly remember in the 1950's being treated to ice-cream in a silver bowl served by Fenwick's waitresses in smart uniforms with white pinafores.

31.(a) Northumberland Street   1897

This view shows the hustle and bustle on the street at the time of Queen Victoria's Diamond Jubilee. Amos Atkinson's boot and shoe shop is well established on the east side of the street. The policeman in the centre of the picture reassures the reader that everything was under control. In the 1937 shot another celebration is taking place as Northumberland Street is decorated with bunting for the coronation of George VI. The photograph shows how inadequate the pavements were, but it was another forty years before they were widened. The old Amos Atkinson's shop is now dwarfed by the surrounding buildings. The shop is still present today but has now changed its name. On the left is the new Monument Mall which replaced the fine stone building which housed Burton the Taylor.

(b) 1937

(c) 1990's

32.(a) New Bridge Street   1895

New Bridge Street was constructed in 1812. The twin-spired church in the centre of the picture is Trinity Presbyterian and next to it is the Unitarian Church of the Divine Unity. On the extreme right is the old Central Library which was built in 1880.

(b) 1987

None of the buildings in the 1895 photograph remains. The new Central Library on the right was constructed in the 1960's and the fine architecture of the churches has been replaced by the hideous block of concrete in the centre.

(c) 1990's

The Burton House pub on the left has gone for a burton and John Dobson Street now extends south to Market Street.

33. Corner Northumberland Street / Blackett Street

(a) 1896

At first sight it would appear that this photograph was taken on a quiet Sunday morning. Closer inspection reveals a ghostly blur along the pavements which indicates that the photograph was taken using a long exposure time and the street was probably as busy as in the other shots.

(b) 1938

The 1938 picture was taken from the balcony of the Paramount cinema (now the Odeon) and shows how busy Northumberland Street used to be. Notice that trams, trolley buses and motor buses were in service simultaneously.

(c) 1953

There was still complete chaos at this junction in 1953 as Northumberland Street had to carry the main north-south trunk traffic as well as local traffic. Cook's corner is seen on the right which took its name from the travel agent's office there. The pavements are filled to capacity; the pedestrians having to pick their way carefully through traffic at the junction.

(d) 1994

Monument Mall now gives a smart new look to the corner. Northumberland Street has been largely pedestrianised and vehicles can now use one of several other routes to avoid this junction. The author would like to thank the manager of the Odeon cinema for allowing him to take this photograph from the cinema's balcony.

34.(a) Pilgrim Street (North)   c.1912

The large white building is Newcastle Conservative Club, a very impressive structure which puts surrounding buildings to shame. The Paramount cinema (now the Odeon) is yet to be built.

(b) 1990's

Today the line of the street has been ruined by the building of an office block which straddles Pilgrim Street. How could planning permission be given for such a monstrosity?

35.(a) Market Street   1905

Market Street was built by Grainger in 1840 and connected Grainger Street to Pilgrim Street. The building on the right is the Central Exchange which was originally built between 1836 and 1838, and then re-built in 1905 after a fire.

(b) 1990's

The Central Exchange's design was based on the Temple of Vesta at Tivoli and was originally planned as a corn market. It now houses the picturesque Central Arcade with banks, shops, and offices. It is the camera lens which is responsible for the buildings' list and not Grainger's workmanship.

36.(a) Grey's Monument   1930

Built in 1838 to commemorate the great work carried out by Charles, Earl Grey on the Reform Bill of 1832. The "Roman Doric Column" stands over 130 ft. high and the statue of Earl Grey faces down the street named after him. The elegant building on the left housed the YMCA and had to give way to the Eldon Square shopping centre.

(b) 1987

By the time of the 1987 photograph, the area around Grey's Monument had been pedestrianised and underneath the column is the Metro underground station which connects two lines of the system.

(c) 1994

The old post office building shown in the previous shot was demolished in order to build Monument Mall which is a splendid piece of architecture in a similar style to buildings erected by Grainger over 100 years ago.

The Friends' Meeting House of the Quaker Movement is shown in the centre of the photograph. Pilgrim Street is being excavated in preparation for the laying of tram lines. The building on the right is the Royal Arcade built by Grainger in 1832.

(b) 1990's

The author would like to thank the Provincial Insurance plc for allowing him to take this shot from the first floor window of their office. Considerably more changes have occurred since the laying of the tram lines and the Quakers have had to find new premises twice since 1900.

38.(a) Pilgrim Street (south)   c.1920

This photograph was taken before the Tyne Bridge was built and so Pilgrim Street is seen to bear left and descend to the river and the Swing Bridge. The shop on the extreme left is Mr Cook's fish and chip saloon and the sign outside Mr Pearson's shop next door enquires "shave sir?"

(b) 1950's

The Tyne Bridge now takes Pilgrim Street's traffic straight across the river. All Saints Church on the left gives travellers a useful time check. The junction of Pilgrim Street with City Road and Mosley street out of view to the left had always been a serious traffic bottleneck. Plans were drawn up for a through-traffic central motor-way with an intersection at this point.

(c) 1990's

The motor-way was completed in 1970 and now takes through-traffic underneath the round-a-bout to the left and out of view of this photograph. A new railway bridge has been built along with a labyrinth of pedestrian tunnels and walkways.

39.(a) Low Pilgrim Street   c.1925

This photograph was taken before the Tyne Bridge was built and Pilgrim Street is seen to descend towards the Quayside passing All Saints Church on the right just out of camera. The men in the centre seem to be waiting for the pub to open on a Sunday morning in true Geordie tradition.

(b) 1960's

The old shops and pubs have almost gone forever and the approach to the Tyne Bridge can be seen with the tower of St. Nicholas' Cathedral just poking above. The Tyne Bridge seems to have made this part of the town appear desolate and neglected.

(c) 1990's

The All Saints office block now dominates the view and obscures the Tyne Bridge. The iron railings remain to convince the doubting viewer that this is the same view.

40.(a) Dog Bank 1   c.1890

Dog bank was a narrow street which ran from Low Pilgrim Street to Broad Chare and passed through the most densely populated area of nineteenth century Newcastle. Notice how the building in the centre appears to be leaning over. The structure was actually built outwards so that the upper floors had a greater floor area to maximise on the space available.

(b) 1987

No one has lived in this part of the City for many decades although building work does appear to be underway.

(c) 1990's

Building work is now complete and Heritage Homes try to encourage citizens to live in the centre of the city once more.

41.(a) Dog Bank 2   c.1890

This is the same street as the previous shot only it is a view looking up the bank. The pub on the right may be the Marquis of Granby.

BROAD GARTH

(b) 1987

(c) 1990's

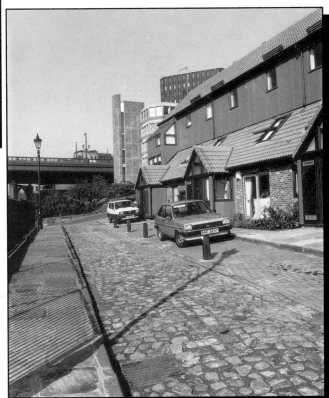

42.(a) Quayside   c.1900

This area had previously been devastated by the great fire of 1854 caused by an explosion in a warehouse across the river in Gateshead. The view shows only two bridges over the Tyne, the High Level Bridge and the Swing Bridge.

(b) 1990's

There are now six bridges from Gateshead to Newcastle, the latest addition being the Queen Elizabeth Bridge carrying Metro trains across the Tyne. The City's new law courts are shown on the right.

43.(a) Ellison Place   1960's

At the turn of the century, Ellison Place was a quiet part of Newcastle which was favoured by the Clergy and assize court judges as a place to reside. The peacefulness of the Square was lost when the gardens in the centre were removed to build a car park.

(b) 1990's

When the Central Motor-way East was completed in 1970, access to Ellison Place was restricted, gardens were planted, and peace was restored once again. The building of Mea House destroyed any charm that remained.

44.(a) Jesmond Road, Jesmond   c.1920

Heavy rainfall caused severe flooding in Jesmond Road at the junction with Shortridge Terrace. The local residents stare in amazement as the waves lap against Mr Elliot's store.

(b) c.1970

The man with the pipe in the early photograph has been replaced by the author's father who surveys the site of the flood over fifty years later.

45.(a) Blue Bell pub, Jesmond Vale   1914

The entire staff and customers of the Blue Bell public house have been talked into standing outside for the photograph. Jesmond Vale school is seen on the left of the picture and the bridge in the foreground crosses the Ouse Burn, a tributary of the River Tyne.

(b) 1990's

The Blue Bell still stands today but the school has been replaced by the Northern Synfonia Centre. Further upstream in Jesmond Vale is Greenwater Pool which was where the annual Newcastle fair called the "Hoppings" was held for a while before it returned to its original venue on the Town Moor.

46.(a) Ouse Burn from Byker Bridge   1961

Further downstream of the Ouse Burn was this part of Byker of which no local could be proud.
Ironically, two miles upstream, is the beautiful parkland of Jesmond Dene, which was a gift to the
City of Newcastle upon Tyne from Lord Armstrong in 1883.

(b) 1990's

By the time of the modern photograph, a breathtaking transformation has taken place. The slums have been demolished, the vale has been landscaped, and the Ouse Burn has been dredged. A new bridge has been built which takes the Metro trains over the vale to Byker.

47.(a) Shields Road, Byker   c.1910

Byker, a suburb of Newcastle, is famous for the Byker Wall, a housing complex built in the 1960's and the subject of much controversy over its aesthetic qualities. This is Shields Road, Byker in 1910, a busy shopping street.

(b) 1990's

The shopping area of Shields Road is still largely intact. The bay windows of the building on the left belong to the Tap and Spile public house which has been fitted out in the style of the period of the 1910 picture.

48.(a) C. A. Parsons Works, Byker   1910

Charles Algernon Parsons, "the man who invented the twentieth century", started his steam turbine manufacturing business in 1889 at Shields Road in Byker. His steam engines were far superior in performance to the traditional reciprocating type and were soon fitted as standard in ships built on the Tyne. By the second photograph, Parsons' steam turbines were being used in many of the world's electric power generating stations. The works have been extended and soon after this shot the buildings in the foreground were demolished to make way for a smart new office block which is shown in the 1990's photograph. Parsons is now part of the Rolls-Royce group of companies and supplies power stations throughout the world with electric power generating equipment.

49.(a) Fox and Hounds Pub, West Road   c.1898

This photograph shows the original Fox and Hounds pub at Benwell Bank Top in about 1898. Two Ball Lonnen is the road seen leading off to the left after the lamp, and on the right are the grounds of West Acres owned by Benjamin Browne, the chairman of Hawthorn Leslie.

(b) 1990's

The new Fox and Hounds was probably built in the 1920's.

50.(a) Denton Burn   c.1900

The West Road or West Turnpike as it was known, runs from Newcastle to Hexham and largely follows the course of the Roman Wall. The views shown here are at Denton Burn looking east towards Newcastle. In the 1940's photograph the old whitewash-walled cottage is still there as are some of the other houses in the distance. There are also links between the 1940's shot and the present day photograph.

(b)1940's

1990's

51.(a) Scotswood Road

This view is at the end of Scotswood Road as it enters the west end of Newcastle. The building with the clock tower is the former cattle market keeper's house which was designed by John Dobson in 1842. Scotswood Road is mentioned in the Tyneside song "The Blaydon Races".

Little has changed in the present-day photograph; the area to the left of the traffic lights is now the Marlborough Crescent bus station.

52.(a) Benwell Village

Benwell, like Elswick, formerly belonged to the Priors of Tynemouth and the old tower of Benwell, which can be seen behind the trees, was used as their summer residence. The building with the hoarding on its roof is the Green Tree public house.

(b) 1990's

Benwell seems to have lost its village character as most of the houses have been converted to business premises.

The Links Between the Photographs

For the benefit of those readers who have not been able to identify the links between the old views and the new, here is a list. The more obvious links are not included. If there is no link then it is stated so, to put the reader out of their misery.

1. Side
The Spirit Vaults lamp bracket at the top left.
5. Westgate Road / Collingwood Street.
The buildings on Collingwood Street.
6. Clayton Street / Pink Lane.
The small building at the extreme left.
9. Fenkle Street.
The four storey building on Clayton Street.
10. Westgate Road.
The windows of the building at the extreme left.
12. Newgate Street.
The IBM building on the left of the 1960's shot.
13. Bigg Market.
Some of the buildings on the left.
14. Newgate Street
The Rose and Crown pub below the Swallow Hotel.
17. Corner Low Friar Street / Newgate Street.
The gable end of the small building on the extreme right.
18. Darn Crook.
The church wall at the bottom right.
19. Top of Darn Crook.
The City Wall at the bottom left.
20. Green Market.
St Andrew's church gateposts on the right.
21. Corner Percy Street / Gallowgate.
The gable end of the shop on the extreme right.
22. Corner Percy Street / Blackett Street.
No link.
23. Corner Percy Street / Gallowgate.
No link.

24. Percy Street.
The Leazes Arcade at the top left.
25. Farmer's Rest.
The shop on the extreme right.
29. Northumberland Road.
The castleated building in the centre.
30. Fenwick's Store.
No link.
31. Northumberland Street.
Amos Atkinson's shop.
32. New Bridge Street.
No link between (a) and (b).
33. Corner Northumberland Street / Blackett Street.
Northern Goldsmith's shop on the left.
34. Pilgrim Street North.
The buildings on the extreme left.
37. Pilgrim Street / Mosley Street.
The Norwich Union building on the left.
38. Pilgrim Street south.
No link between (a) and (b).
40. Dog Bank.
The curve of the kerb on the right.
41. Dog Bank
The number of cobble stones.
43. Ellison Place.
The block of flats on the left.
50. Denton Burn.
The cottage on the left and other buildings along the West Road.
52. Benwell Village.
The house on the extreme left.

Acknowledgements

The author would like to thank Craig Oliphant for taking the new photographs and printing some of the very old negatives of the early views. Thanks also go to the staff of Newcastle Central Library Local Studies Department for their help in the research work and thank you to Horsley Hall for checking the script.

Further Reading

Tyneside: Past and Present
A Journey Through Time and Tyneside by Geoff Phillips

Tyneside: Past and Present is in the same format as this book with old and new views side by side of Newcastle, its suburbs, and Tyneside towns and villages. In many cases there are hidden links between the old and new views which are fun to find.

- The Blaydon Races Procession on Collingwood Street, 1901.

- The North-East Coast Exhibition at Newcastle in 1929.

- Cullercoats fishermen launch their boats at Cullercoats railway station to rescue stranded passengers in the flood of 1900.

- The three ships of Whitley Bay; three different Ship Hotels in the same spot but separated in time by almost 100 years.

- The first electric train on the coast line; 1904.

- The opening of the Coast Road in 1927.

Over 100 photographs of Tyneside as it used to be alongside views of the present day. Intriguing facts and information about each photograph along with a descriptive journey around Tyneside which shows the reader the views in the order as they appear in the book. 108 pages, paperback. ISBN 0 9522480 0 X.

Obtainable where you bought this book.

Published and distributed by G.P. Electronic Services, (091) 384 9707